Under Cornflower Blue Skies

Poems

John T. Bensing

ISBN   978-0-9991097-0-0
           978-0-9991097-1-7
           978-0-9991097-2-4

Cover photo: John T. Bensing
Author photo: Signature Studios

Printed in the USA on acid-free paper.

Author inquiries, online and mail orders:
            johntbensing@gmail.com

Acknowledgements

Heartfelt gratitude to Jean Wolph, director of the Louisville Writing Project. Jean patiently nurtured the poet in me. She is a brilliant and inspirational teacher. I'm proud to call her my mentor. Thank you, Tim Johnson, for your early and continued support as a teacher, fellow writer, and editor. Also, thanks to Elizabeth Dick, Holly Fink, Aretha Whaley, and Evan Payne. Thank you to all who have read and listened. My wife, Mary, deserves a special mention for editing, typing, and bringing this work to press.

Contents

Contents

for my wonderful family

SCISSORS

Anna is wearing her cartoon dress,
the pink one she sleeps in.
A crocheted scarf the length of her body
trails from her neck. Today she is Rapunzel
standing high on the arm of the chair
letting down her hair. She skips
across the back of the couch where she gazes
out the picture window
into a forest only she can see.

When summer is over, she will go to kindergarten.
She will not wear her Disney gown or plastic tiara.
They will cure her imagination
with a, e, i, o, u, and take away two.
She will learn to walk in silent lines in the halls
and eat her lunch in twenty minutes.
Her sprite spirit will be broken.
They will turn her into a "big girl."
And I will never be the same.

POTTING SHED

In coat and scarf, I go to the potting shed,
to fill bird feeders with black oil
sunflower seed and sit
watching dark clouds
press down on the roof
of my house as its chimney
exhales white wisps.

No reason to rearrange
the garden tools again,
testing for sharpness,
checking for rust,
except for the pleasure
of holding them in my hands.

If there is enough day left,
I dig into bags of potting soil
up to my elbows
and gather crescents of black
under my fingernails.
After dinner, the television
blurts bad news
and the dishwasher churns.

I come to sit in the dark with my pipe,
blow rings around the full moon,
and inhale the smoke
of neighbors' hearths.
If I draw slowly,
I can plant the whole spring garden
in an evening.

MILKWEED IN WINTER

Brittle milkweed vines are woven
through a garden trellis.
Seeds with gossamer white tails
parachute from a cracked fuselage.
The wind catches them like sails.

Leaning in, I shiver
in a one-inch depth of field,
twisting the lens and tripping
the shutter until I'm sure
I've captured an early flight to spring.

Winter Mornings

Like salt from a shaker,
white crystals fall
from a pewter-colored sky.
Worker bees in frigid cars
puff invisible cigarettes
willing the red needle to move
so they can clear windshields
and feel their feet and hands.

ZONE 5 LATE MARCH

Warm days like these,
we ignore the calendar.
On our knees, we sprinkle
bulbs with bone meal,
fill holes and cover beds
with chicken wire
to keep squirrels out.

We stash flats of tomato
plants in dark garages
and wonder why they die.
Growers laugh behind our backs
and sell them to us twice.

Spring fever's pockets are deep.
Call it romance. Call it disease.
It starts in February,
mailboxes stuffed
with catalogs of blossoms.

We take them to bed with us,
lusting after form and color...
> *up to 20 tangerine colored*
> *blooms with little freckles,*
> *extremely recurved petals*
> *and stamens that look like*
> *long eyelashes!*

Description lulls us to sleep.
We dream of our home in Eden.

CATCH AND RELEASE

The Styrofoam bobber floats motionless
like Earth in the atlas at home,
forever fixed in two dimensions, between
winter and spring.

Impatient, I pick up the camera
and catch cirrus clouds brushed
luminous white above the horizon,
a fog bank burning off mountain tops
the color of my beard,
and loons diving for fish off the point.

These in my creel, I cast my line again.

The great fish buries the bobber,
pulling the rod tip under the boat.
I fumble to loosen the drag,
give her more line,
let her run,
tire her out.
I raise the rod overhead,
glimpse the bronze wobble and orange eye.
She bends the rod willow again,
peels four-pound test and dives for darkness.

The Earth hurtles toward the equinox.
Forsythia blossoms in my backyard.
Honeysuckle wafts through windows
over Chattanooga.

I guide her in.
The fly falls from her small mouth.
She is slippery and wet like my firstborn child,
and I thrust her toward the camera,
adding weight and girth
to the first of many stories I will tell.

STRATUS CLOUDS

Standing in the shadow
of the dark barn,
I blow clouds across a mug
of black coffee.
No god again today.
He is covered by a species
of clouds that overstay their welcome
and infect my altitude.

They wrestle me to the ground,
suck moisture from my shell
and spit it back in my face.
I watch them grumble away
east towards April and May.

Knowing: in time a flock
of sheep will convene
in a high blue pasture,
and horses, too,
galloping steadfast
chasing a setting sun.

MY WEATHER GIRL

She was predictable,
always blowing in.
When she slept over
she'd wedge her frigid
body under mine
until I rose for blankets.
She woke in a fog,
frosty at breakfast.

If she stayed,
she was cooler the second day.
This natural procession
always evoked a thrill in her.
If she couldn't raise a thunderhead,
she'd pout and cry big tears:
whistling and moaning at turns
until the water cycle was complete.

COME MARCH

Come March,
when the stone rolls away,
and I look you in the eye again,
golden streams of light
will fill my irises with hope.
Your blue transparent wash of sky
will raise sweet green fescue
high enough to blow into windrows.
Winter hands blister
until they remember
the rhythm of the rake again.
Tines will turn and the fragrance of loam
will fill me with garden faith.
At the end of the day,
I'll taste salt on my skin
for the first time this year.
I'll fold green stained hands
and praise you for the sun.

CAROLINA WILD PETUNIA

Field guide in hand,
I wade a wet, grassy meadow
that cups the pond
and discover, deep in green,
a *blue-violet* flower
that ducked the mower.

I pick the blossom,
memorize its hue,
find its photograph.

I spin it between finger and thumb
blurring its radial symmetry,
seeing it Monet,
and for a moment

I am Adam
naming the flora of Eden.

EARLY THIS MORNING

A five-alarm bladder
wakes me at four-forty-five.
The low-pressure stream
starts-stops-spits in the bowl.
Outside, airbrakes hiss and screech,
closer and closer, house to house.

Still comatose, I sprint,
dragging trash to the street.
Just in time.
Men in neon vests applaud,
whistling at my wife's robe
and kitty-cat slippers.
Cat-calls echo down the block.

LARGEMOUTH BASS 6 LBS. 2 OZ.
for Josh

From the opposite bank,
I watched the lightning twist
of his upper body set the hook.
Reflex: eyes, brain, hands,
fingers reeling slack.
He pointed the rod
at the thrashing wake
and waited to feel the fish,
just like I'd taught him.

Unable to resist the vibration
of the paddling feet and side
to side swagger of the lure,
the fooled fish mauled
the white plastic frog.
An electric number six
meat hook did her in.

Even from across the pond,
before the fish was landed:
before the scale, the pictures,
the lies, the smart aleck retort.
(*My work is done here*).
I knew it was a trophy.

INTERSPECIES DATING

for composers Ahbez and Cole

I brought Rose Begonia home
two years ago
where she didn't do well
as an annual in the front
bed with the other girls.

I grew weary of her diva nature
and incessant bitching
about a pink German who called her a harlot
when she played The Green House.
We grew estranged but I missed her.

I saw her again this spring,
flamboyant as usual
tossing her floribunda red head
above a table of early girls and better boys:
common vegetables she called them.

She said she'd come back
if I'd guarantee a gig
on the screened porch
and lavish her with saucers
of Monty's Joy Juice.
Too weak to resist
her colored wigs and cancan foliage,
I picked her up.

Evenings on the porch
Rosie performs musical selections
from Moulin Rouge
and sits with me between sets.
She calls me Nature Boy and croons:

The greatest thing
you'll ever learn
is just to love
and be loved in return.

SOFT WHITE PETALS

for Jessica

The dog who lay
on my chest,
her body rising and falling
while I counted breaths
in prayer and meditation
was burned to ash—
the color of her coat.

In October,
I sprinkled her ashes
around a *jane magnolia*
beneath my window.
Now she sleeps curled
in tightly wrapped buds.

When spring comes
I will cup flowers
in my hands
and stroke her
soft white petals.

SUN, MOON, AND STARS

The dandelion on the horizon
has dimmed and gone to seed,
rising in darkness, blown
into a billion winter nightlights.

DOES IT MAKE YOU SAD?

In Autumn,
when you walk the forest,
can you call the trees by name?
Do they speak to you
as you wade their brittle cast-off masks?

Can you close your eyes,
run your fingers across their skin
and whisper, *I know you?*

Can you resist climbing
high with the faith of a child
swaying in the blue,
surveying the whole forest,
as close to God
as you ever have been?

Have you buried yourself
lying perfectly still
beneath their leaves,
hiding yourself
from every living thing,
inhaling the earth,
pretending to die,

only to be awakened
by the scratchy rhythm
of rakes on pavement?

And does it make you sad
to see the party
all cleaned up–
confetti stuffed in plastic bags,
set out on the curb,
as if it were only trash?

END OF THE ROLL

On September twenty-second
the calendar cautions us
like a check engine light.
Kodachrome days are over.

There are only two seasons
summer and winter,
light and dark.
Fall is the mourning period.

Harvesting of serotonin begins.
Thanksgiving and Christmas—
merciful distractions
along the path of black ice

on the way to the cold storage
of January and February.
Numbing of the neocortex makes us forget
there is still a sun above the clouds.

By spring, tapped and drained
like sugar maples,
all but our essence is boiled down.
Finally, forsythia saves us.

ADULTS WILL TELL YOU PLUTO'S NOT A PLANET

but I've been there.
One Saturday, when I was nine,
I visited Pluto in a rocket
made from a refrigerator box.
I drew the instrument panel
with Magic Markers.

Neighbor kids paid me a dime
for a window seat.
We blasted off from the driveway
flight after flight
all day long
till night fell.

That night there was a ring
around the moon
and it rained.
Next morning,
the nose cone was mushy,
the hatch wouldn't seal,
and my friend, John Sullivan,
(who got A's in Science)
told the whole neighborhood:
>   the structural integrity of his rocket
>   is compromised.
>   That craft is unsafe and will never survive
>   the g-forces to leave earth's atmosphere again.
After that,
no one would fly with me,
not even for the reduced fare of a nickel.
The mission was scrubbed.

I cried the day Dad
sliced up my ship with a box cutter
and piled it out on the curb
with the trash.

That night, after dark,
I managed to salvage
the instrument panel
and hide it under my mattress.

I still have it.

GIVE A KID A BOX
for Holly

A friend of mine, when she was eight,
ran a cardboard pirate ship aground
in an alley behind her house.
Many of her friends went down that day,
so she gathered a crew from a block away,
salvaged the wreck and built a stage,
so that her lost mates could have a part
in a production of Macbeth.
Parents gathered every night,
while flashing bugs in mason jars
lit up the great white way,
and after each performance,
she made a plea:
Somebody, please buy a refrigerator
so we can have the box.

A NOTE FROM ART CLASS

I borrowed your basket,
the one I made in Santa Fe,
where I learned I am not a weaver,
and the stoneware cup and saucer
we only use at Thanksgiving.
I took the matching creamer, too.
No need to look for the crystal
salt and pepper shakers, or the blue
granite pitcher we use for tea.

My third-grade artists
are drawing a still-life this week.
They wanted to come to our kitchen,
but I said no. Still they wonder
what you look like, and how hard it will be
to draw your salt-and-pepper hair
and round Irish face.
I have promised to pose you with
a cup of tea, in your favorite flannel gown,
the comfy one with the holes.

IN THE ART ROOM

Pencils get
shorter
every day,
morphed
into
spiral
shavings.
Children
unravel
pictures
and
poems,
leaving
lines and shapes
on pure white
sulphite
that may not
survive
the bus ride
home
to
live
for a time
on the Frigidaire.

THE POTTER

Muddy of mind, the potter returns to his wheel
resolved to reverse billions of years of erosion.
He plunges fingers and hands into spinning earth,
feels it crack his skin, grind his nails,
finally yield and center in his slippery wet grip.

Particles, small as motes of dust, reunite
like his own genes, rising into forms
as if he were father to bottle and bowl,
vessels with feet, shoulders, lips and mouths
to bear the soul of their maker, drunk with spinning.

WHY I WILL NOT DRIVE
For Mary

It is only in the car
the conversation continues,
because she cannot drive and read

the book wrapped with the ripped
half-naked man, his tender touch
on the heroine's shoulder,
her eyes closed in ecstasy.

This is when we talk
of children, coupons, unpaid bills,
how cold a king-size bed can be.

CENOTE

It is a short flight from Cincinnati
to the Mexican Riviera.
My wife sits by the window
pointing out angels in the clouds.
I dodge carts of nuts and drinks.

She will never forget this trip
I promised her.
She thinks we are going to the beach.
I will show her Maya
today and yesterday.

I planted this homecoming
like grains of maize
in the fertile wanderlust of her mind.
I was a patient farmer,
and now she will see the harvest.

I will show her who owns the sky.

The photographs will picture a step pyramid,
me at the top, arms outstretched,
reclaiming my city on the sea.
Clouds in the background
snub hills of beans and squash,
threatening to abandon sweet corn.

If it is her time,
I need not even nick her with the obsidian blade.
If her blood does not bring the rain,
we will swim in the cenote.
I will show her the deep underwater caves.

SMALL WORLD

I've been to Disney's World.
It's not so magic after dark.
After the fireworks display,
people trudge miles back to their cars
to find they've left lights on.

Heat hangs over an asphalt ocean of mini-vans.
Tow trucks jump dead batteries.
Families shuffle and mumble
like spectators at an accident scene.
Kids, sugared up on blue and purple slush
from cartoon character cups,
know the mouse is dead—
for at least another year.

Dad looks down at his feet,
rattling loose change,
thinking the money spent
could have bought a bass boat,
knowing at six a.m.
he'll be fighting the assembly line
in Tomorrow Land.

Mom's jouncing a whiny baby on her hip,
too tired to pay for this tonight,
praying he showers first.

Back at the park,
an oily faced kid peels off a Goofy mask
and wonders if he's got a shot
at screwing Snow White
before summer is gone.

THE TIN MAN

He was happy to measure,
cut and build boxes from
sheets of metal–
duct work that moved fresh air.

He loved when Mom said,
My Sheet Metal Man is home.

He learned he'd have to follow
the work to make a living
for Mom and us four kids
so, he went inside

to work for Mr. Ford.

Cars got faster
and so did the line,
ten-hour days
six days a week.

Dad never meant to settle.

Somewhere in Tomorrow Land
the *Tin Man* lost his heart.
There was no wizard at our house,
so, we lived with a *Body Man*
who worked for Mr. Ford.

Hell, we all worked for Mr. Ford.

THE UNMADE BED

Where is the virtue
in making a bed?
You'll only sleep in it again.
As if you lived
at Bed Bath and Beyond,
where beds (without mattresses)
display spreads,
dust ruffles,
printed sheets,
quilts and comforters
(which somehow
seem the same).

No, I prefer
the honesty
of the unkempt
snowy landform
of an unmade bed;
ripples of white
foothills
stretching end to end
and at higher
elevations,
two mountains
with a valley
in-between.

NIGHT FISHING BELOW THE HYDROELECTRIC PLANT

Beneath a white churning torrent,
long silver stripers
gather in dark current
like a pack of wolves,

waiting for the turbine to inhale
unsuspecting flashes,
blend them into chum
and spit them into
gaping mouths.

We stand small
on the bank
gripping lightning rods
strung with heavy line
pointing them toward heaven
with both hands

guiding buck-tails
through mean current,
bouncing them off concrete,
rebar, and rip-rap;
casting into the fray
again and again.

FISHING WITH POP
for Cooper

Someday I'll get lost again,
in east Tennessee,
along 25/70,
where it narrows
to one lane.

I'll take your fly rod and cast
behind boulders,
where water swallows
the voices of campers
tending cook fires.

I'll tighten drag
on one last trout,
wait for the dipper,
then pour coffee
black as a new moon.

GUARDRAIL LULLABY

Rivers and streams
cross the TripTik™
like a patchwork
of varicose veins.
Headlights grow from
when-you-wish-upons
to meteoric head-ons.

No amount of smoke and joe
will pull back the blanket
that tucks in East and West,
so you chase the red tails
of eighteen-wheelers
and stay on your side
of a broken white line

racing through states
of semi-consciousness,
lulled by the fading static
of a dying radio
and signs that blink
No Vacancy.

BOTH SIDES NOW
for Joni

Slowly, in her signature cigarette timbre
she rises, taking the orchestra with her.
We are cumulus and she is the breeze.
Joni sings with her whole body,
delicately moving arms, hands, fingers,
as if to feel our faces.

Cellists draw their bows.
Our hearts are easy marks.

A tuxedo playing a muted trumpet rises
and carries her to the last verse,
tongue kissing her with a sensuous solo.
They finish together.

The crowd rises and thunder cracks
all over the auditorium.
I wipe tears from my face.
I really don't know why.

FROM THE CLICHÉ CAFÉ

If this pen and paper could speak,
they'd say, we missed you
and the fine cursive pressure
you put on us to carry
your words into the world.

I would apologize and say,
I've returned to be the scribe
for the mind that stands
on the shoulders of others
who trusted them with secrets and songs.

I would tell the flowing ink and stuff of trees
I am back to prove myself
to an audience who is nearly deaf
to cadence and rhythm,
that my subconscious has not
resolved her identity crisis,

how I missed traveling without a map
to places where only the muse
can connect synapse to synapse.
As darkness fell on the cliché café,
I would swallow the last of my raspberry latte,
cap the pen and close the journal.

ARCADIA

These fresh words,
written and mouthed one time.
What happens to them now,
and what of their meanings?
Before their ink was dry,
I loved them.
Now they are printed, stacked, and stapled.
Do their syllables roll
and bounce against bumpers
in the electric skull:
finally ringing bells and racking up points
before a new spring-loaded one
is pulled with hopeful fingers
and shot into this guessed-at-world?

READING AT THE BAR

For Evan

Poetry shirts are available at the door.
You don't have to wear them in public.
You can sleep in one.
I won't out anybody.
No one will know you were here.

Tonight, before you close your eyes,
remember how you chased
a favorite line with a beer,
and how, for a moment,
we shared a lifeboat, laughing.

FALL FISHING WITH YOU
for Skeeter

Remember when we sat in silence
and cast our lures into the slow
moving mountains of cumulus clouds
and waited for the full moon to rise
and cross the dam.

Fishing was slow and you whispered
a lesson in botany, pointing out
purple ironweed on the bank,
and yellow primrose floating below us.
We listened to hedge apples bounce
and roll through underbrush.

We waited for our lines to twitch
and when we were quick enough
buck bass performed aerial acts
and tail-walked across the glass
before we released them back into the deep.

MAX

The Yorkshire terrier
who migrated
from yard to house,
more monarch than mongrel,
has enthroned himself
on the upholstered chair
beside the picture window.
The sheers are shredded
and the window bears
the smudge of his nose.
More greeter than guard,
he is not a lap dog.
Weary of rawhide,
he cuts his teeth
on my wife's kitchen chair.
He has been known
to dance for a treat,
something my wife has never done.

CHRISTMAS PRESENT

Christmas Eve: two generations rolled
in like a tsunami, shredding wrapping paper,
piling plunder, leaving the smallest lost,
awash in discovery and awe.

The wave continued into the kitchen
consuming honey baked ham,
whipped potatoes and dressing, slow cooked
green beans with onions and bacon, butternut
squash, baked sweet potatoes and marshmallows,
cranberry apple sauce, and yeast rolls.

Today Nana and Grumps cradle
warm cups of coffee, sitting close
behind a camera, savoring
scenes of exquisite chaos,
waiting for the lunch crowd.

The fridge is stuffed with left-overs;
every inch of counter top crowded
with foil covered desserts.

Before the year is over, we will simmer
ham, bone, and beans, and argue
who makes the best bean soup.
We will clink wine glasses and toast
our short-lived decadence.

MOTHER'S TURBAN

She shows me
the plastic bag of hair
that fell in handfuls
after her last treatment.
It looks like batting
from one of her quilts.
I want it
but haven't the courage to ask.
We don't talk about why
she's keeping it.
The blonde wig was free, she says,
and doesn't itch much.
So, do blondes really have more fun, I ask?
Not lately, she says.
I tell her it looks fine.
In truth, it doesn't match
her pale features.
Next, she models a colorful turban.
They sell you a crystal ball with that?
My second failed joke
and the heat rises
in my neck and face.
She pulls my hand up under the headdress,
makes me feel the resurrection of fine hair.
I don't need a crystal ball.

THE TACKLE BOX YOU LEFT ME

I wanted more than the boxful
of plastic lures and hooks.

You never understood my every cast
to tempt you into conversation.

You never sensed the yards of axon curling
high in the blue behind me, then unrolling

to the synapse between us,
floating like sun on water.

I watched the ripples dissipate
and you, like God, never took the bait.

BREAKFAST WITHOUT HER

I remove foil
from cold
baked potatoes,
and slice them
thin as poker chips–
arrange them
in the sizzling oil
in her cast iron skillet.
I wash down pills
with raspberry coffee
and debate whether
to shower and dress,
or burrow back
under quilts
she left me.

YOU ALL GO ON WITHOUT ME

I was nine when Dad got the call
from the shotgun house
in the west end of town,
the house with the unmade bed
and rosary beads
strewn on crumpled sheets.

Tom, we're at Mom's dividing up her stuff.
There must be something you want.
Are you sure you can't come down?
She had a note in her purse your Johnny wrote her.
No telling how long she's carried it around.

No, you all go on without me.

And I never got a thing,
just the death card at the funeral home
and the few stories I could pry out of Dad
those Christmases when we left a wreath
on Grandma's grave.

When I went to my cousins' houses after that,
I saw bits and pieces of Grandma–
the washstand with the marble top,
the bas-relief of the Lion of Lucerne,
and the family photographs.

I am forty-six and I still respect Dad's decision
to step back from the fray,
but even now,
when I visit Aunt Mary's and see the washstand,
I want that note they found in Grandma's purse.

CONCERNING THE QUILTS YOU LEFT US

*In some cultures, people believe their ancestors
possess power to intervene in their lives, aiding or
punishing them for misdeeds.*

I imagine you, needle in hand,
sewing stitches fast and close,
no fear of a deadline,
just for the pleasure of it.

I run upstairs
where your great-grandbabies sleep,
your rose print quilt lies
crumpled on the floor,
the blue ribbon lost.
I shake it open over the bed.
It hovers, floats, settles.
I smooth wrinkles
with both hands,
checking for pins.

PARTING WORDS FOR GROWN CHILDREN

I will not keep you long.
I doubt I will leave you much
more than a fading memory,
a box of fishing lures,
my orchid collection,
and a shelf of books
on how to write a poem.

By the time these lines make sense
you will write your own,
spiral bound and in your head,
taking turns at art and instinct,
no longer seeking my approval.

If your children grow curious,
there is a carousel of Kodachrome
in the top of the closet,
slides of a wedding in seventy-eight.
We loved each other, hated each other,
and loved each other again.
Your mother loved you more.

Do not search my journals
for wisdom or secrets.
My words were white ash
you scattered with the rest of me
at Paradise Falls.
Everyone's secrets are the same—
our pain and happiness—
all the same.

You may summon me in a dream
when you have forgotten your way:
I left you answers
in a box of fishing lures,
my orchid collection,
and a shelf of books
on how to write a poem.

RAINY DAY FRIENDS

Don't abandon rainy day friends
who hide behind a cold front
and cover Sun and Moon,

who live in stratus altitudes
and yearn for the clearing
of a sunny cumulus day.

Be there when they rise and rain.
Be there for their thunderhead.
Stay and dodge their hailstones.

Above all, don't look down
from your wispy cirrus height.
We all live at the whim of the wind.

I KNOW

My wife's children were home.
We shared dinner,
pork barbeque prepared by the boys,
slow cooked in crockpots.

We filled two tables
with laughter, bad jokes, and gossip.
After supper we fought over
who would buy the ice cream.

My wife is still full from their visit,
and may not eat for days.
She is sated by their parting embraces,
new loves, new jobs, even their pain.

I am alone
with half empty soda cans,
a sink of dishes,
and the white noise
of the ceiling fan.

How can you still be hungry, she asks,
as I savor the last of the pork
and wash it down with a lone beer.
They love you, too, she says.

I know.

MAKEUP

The poison
that keeps
my lymph nodes
from swelling
marks my face
with bloody blotches.
I dab them
with a stick of concealer
close as I can match
to my natural color,
and blend the edges
with a soft, bristled brush.
On close observation
the makeup is visible,
but people have stopped
narrowing their eyes
when they are in my space.
Better to be thought vain than pitied.

STUFF

Dear Mom and Dad,

I think about you every evening
when I turn the night light
on inside the china lamp you left.

I think about you when I pass crates
stuffed with photos
you were too busy living to label.

And I realize my stuff
will get the same attention
from my children when I pass.

They will think of us every evening
when they turn the night light
on inside the china lamp you left.

QUILTERS AT BLUE LICKS BATTLEFIELD

A crazy quilt of colored leaves
covers rolling hills around the lodge.
Inside, the women do the work
they have always done,
whispering quiet as thread
pulled through fabric.

They share and sew
their secrets between
colorful tops and backing.
They continue an unbroken
running stitch that holds
their lives, their families,
themselves together.

Men build and rip apart,
but in the dark their women,
quilters ever mindful,
know we will all lie together
layer upon layer
stitched, pieced, and bound
by those who forever
bear and comfort us.

GLOW WORMS

The miracle is not
the blinking bugs,
but shadows
shrieking in delight,
running with glowing jars.

My children cannot know
the light I gather
nor, how like glow worms,
I too will return
to sleep beneath the grass.

MOTHER'S DREAM

For Paige

How can we grieve
wrapped in the quilts
we watched you sew?

On cold nights, my wife
pulls Flying Geese across me
and claims it as her own.

Your great-grandchildren
make tents and read stories
under Big Dipper.

How can we grieve
when you stitched
layers like generations
and swaddle us still?

AT THE PUMPKIN PATCH

Six-year-old Anna sits at the wheel
of the tractor. It's her turn to drive.
Hands at three and nine.
Her eyes are focused on pumpkins
all the way to the horizon
under a cornflower blue sky.
She wears a fixed stare
and a baby teeth smile.
The tractor never moves,
but Anna is long gone.

THE CANDLE

When he drank,
he thought of her.
At night, he left
a window open,
lit a candle
and watched moths
circle the flame.
In the morning,
I cleaned them
off the nightstand
and cried.

www.ingramcontent.com/pod-product-compliance
Lightning Source LLC
Chambersburg PA
CBHW031614040426
42452CB00006B/516